Published in the United States of America by The Child's World®
PO Box 326 • Chanhassen, MN 55317-0326
800-599-READ • www.childsworld.com

My First Steps to Math™ is a registered trademark of Scholastic, Inc.

Library of Congress Cataloging-in-Publication Data
Moncure, Jane Belk.
My two book / by Jane Belk Moncure.
p. cm. — (My first steps to math)
ISBN 1-59296-657-8 (lib. bdg. : alk. paper)
1. Counting—Juvenile literature. 2. Number concept—Juvenile literature. I. Title.
QA113.M6687 2006
513.2'11—dc22
2005025692

My two Book

by Jane Belk Moncure

illustrated by Kate Flanagan

This is Little two.

Little  lives in the house of two.

It has two rooms. Count them. One. Two.

Every day Little  two puts on her . . .

two shoes

and goes for a walk.

One day, she found

two caterpillars.

Every day, the caterpillars changed a little.

Until one day, they grew . . .

into two butterflies!

One.   Two.

How many butterflies flew away?

Little two clapped two claps. Can you?

Little 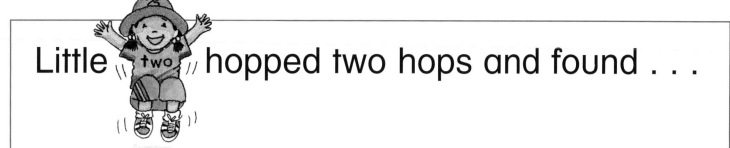 hopped two hops and found . . .

two hens.

The hens said,
Cluck, cluck
two times. Can you?

Then the hens flew away.

Little **two** saw two eggs.

Guess what?

The eggs cracked open!

Out hopped two little chicks.
The chicks said, *Peep, peep*
two times. Can you?

How many baby chicks went hop, hop?

Later, Little  found two lambs.

The lambs were sad. "We are lost," they said.

"We want our mamas!"

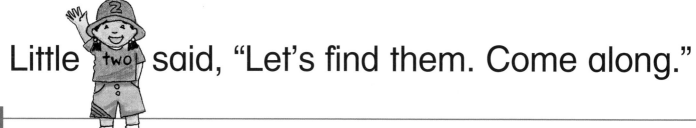

Little two said, "Let's find them. Come along."

Little **two** found one . . .

mama sheep.

How many mamas were still missing?

Little two found the other mama sheep.

How many animals
are in the pen?

Next Little two found . . .

two tadpoles.

She put the two tadpoles in a bowl.

She waited two weeks. Guess what?

The tadpoles grew into frogs.

How many?

Little  two said, "Hop! Hop!"

The two frogs went hop, hop. Can you?

Then Little two saw . . .

two stars in the sky.

One.  Two.

"I must go home," Little  said.

She yawned two yawns. Can you?

She took off two shoes. One. Two.
Then she found . . .

two teddy bears

and two blankets.

Little  two hopped—one, two—into bed . . .

and went to sleep in two winks.

Little  finds two of everything.

two caterpillars 　　two eggs

two butterflies　　two chicks

two hens 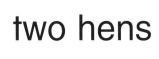　　two lambs

two sheep  two stars

two tadpoles   two teddy bears

two frogs

Now you find two things.

Let's add with Little  .

   +   =

2   +   0   =   2

   +      =

I   +   I   =   2

Now take away.

2   –   1   =   1

2   –   0   =   2

Little **two** makes a 2 this way:

Then she makes the number word like this:

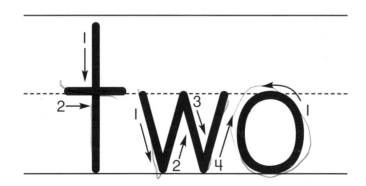

You can make them in the air with your finger.